Letting Go

Thirty Mourning Sonnets
and two poems

Josephine Balmer

AGENDA EDITIONS

ISBN 978-1-908527-29-5

Published in 2017 by
Agenda Editions
The Wheelwrights
Fletching Street
Mayfield
East Sussex
TN20 6TL

Design and production by JAC design
Crowborough, East Sussex

Printed and bound in Great Britain by
TJ International Ltd, Padstow, Cornwall

for Darlene Balmer

Also by Josephine Balmer:

Sappho: Poems & Fragments
Classical Women Poets
Catullus: Poems of Love and Hate
Rearranging the World: A contemporary anthology of literature in translation (ed.)
Chasing Catullus: Poems, Translations & Transgressions
The Word for Sorrow
Piecing Together The Fragments: Translating Classical Verse, Creating Contemporary Poetry
The Paths of Survival

Josephine Balmer's latest collections include *The Paths of Survival* (Shearsman, 2017), *The Word for Sorrow* (Salt, 2013) and *Chasing Catullus: Poems, Translations & Transgressions* (Bloodaxe, 2004). She has also translated Sappho, Classical Women Poets and Catullus, all for Bloodaxe. Her study of classical translation and poetic versioning, *Piecing Together The Fragments*, was published by Oxford University Press in 2013. Single poems and translations have appeared in many publications including *Agenda, Arion, Horizon, The Independent, The Independent on Sunday, Long Poem Magazine, Modern Poetry in Translation, New Statesman, The Observer* and *The Wolf,* and been anthologised widely as well as broadcast on many radio and TV programmes. She writes on poetry and translation for several newspapers and journals including *TLS, New Statesman* and *The Times*, for which she sets the daily Word Watch and weekly Literary Quiz. She studied Classics and Ancient History at University College, London, and was awarded a PhD in Literature and Creative Writing by the University of East Anglia. She lives on the edge of the Ashdown Forest, East Sussex, with her husband, the journalist Paul Dunn, and one dog.

http://thepathsofsurvival.wordpress.com/

Acknowledgements:

Most of these poems have previously been published in *Agenda*.
'Lost' and 'Let Go' also appear in the forthcoming *Virgil and his Translators* edited by Susanna Braund & Zara Torlone (Oxford University Press).
Some of the sonnets were presented at the 'Remaking ancient Greek and Roman myths in the twenty-first century' colloquium at the Open University London Centre in July 2016, and at the 'Lyric and Lyricism' event at Ertegun House, University of Oxford, in September 2016.

Sincere thanks are due to Patricia McCarthy, Paschalis Nikolaou, Fiona Cox, Elena Theodorakopoulos, Fiona Macintosh, Stephanie Oade, Emma Bridges and Susan Bassnett for their much-appreciated support of these poems. They also could not have been written without the love and support of my family: my father Ted Balmer, my sister Teresa Trangmar and, as always, my husband Paul Dunn.

Contents

The Front Cover image is from the etching 'Kiss' by Rachael Kantaris, used by kind permission of the artist.

Things We Leave Behind

after Cavafy

We knew it at once: the faded grooves
touched by the afternoon sun.
The crack where we'd left it too long
in the window, splitting the wood in two.
The candle wax we'd scrubbed but not removed.

Ah, yes, this table, it *was* our family.

We'd seen it last in the van from the charity,
shrouded by its empty, upturned chairs.
Now here it was in the newly-opened café
(had it been an office? No, the bakers...);
a resting-place for dust-blanched builders
slumped over strong tea, the full English,
as dark and heady as funeral incense.

They will always be around somewhere,
those worn-out things we leave behind...

On the other side, the place where she laughed
every birthday, all those festive lunches.
In the centre, the faint circle of a wine glass
abandoned to carry in warmed plates or dishes,
indelible now, an ever-bleeding blemish.

That afternoon, at 4 o'clock, we said goodbye
for one week only... I thought I'd see her.
And then that week became forever.

Lost

after Virgil

Up to that point, I was still in the dark.
I was retracing steps, staring down paths
I saw as ours, not thinking she had been
ripped from us already, had slipped unseen
as she sat down to rest. We'd just spoken –
I heard her laughing, hanging up the phone –
but when next we gathered, friends, family,
one of us would be missing, tricked away.
I bargained with gods I did not worship;
I blamed, I begged ambulance men, medics.
Reaching home, I tried to put on armour,
convincing myself that they had saved her,
that they had been in time, they had, they had...
In response there was only silence, dread.

Suppliants

ghosting Aeschylus

They had laid her out like a warrior,
placed a hand towel under slippered feet,
a doormat for head, shielded by her hair.
I knelt beside her, too soon yet to weep,
and, like a suppliant, I took her hand,
told her she was beautiful, loved, would be
always. This had been our sanctuary
but now we were fugitives, shored on land
we no longer knew. Now we spoke only
in laments, the savage language of hurt,
strangeness of mourning. Up ahead was dust,
the dirt cloud of an advancing army,
a whirl of axles churning up soft earth –
ruthless, muffled. And already on us.

iii

Ring

for Dad

The last time he had held it in his hands
was Penzance, late nineteen-fifty-five. Storms
that roared around the church had for once ebbed;
coats were being unbuttoned, wool scarves shed.
Outside, my beaming mother had just stepped
from the car, poised between past life and next,
as the weight of a box in his best suit
became a bond, unbroken, resolute.

Tonight he twists it between taut fingers,
peering through its opened circle as if
a peephole into some new dimension
where all the days and years might not have been.
The door chimes: undertakers at the gate.
Now there's just one vow left for him to make.

iv

To-Do

Decide sandwiches for the caterers.
Get order of service to the printer.
Look out a photo for cover picture.
Talk to the priest about bidding prayers.
Draw a map for non-local travellers.
List B'n'Bs for those who stay over.
Organise cars for family mourners.
Choose a coffin from the undertakers.

Sort her notes by the side of the cooker.
File shopping never bought, chores for later.
Read a life scribbled on scraps of paper.
Find that last To-Do, scrawled to comfort her:
Walk on cliff tops covered with spring flowers.
Trace her *Heaven on earth.* Fading. Fainter.

V

Halcyon

after Ovid

I remember the times I'd bustled on,
oblivious; doing the chores, piling
up my best clothes, folding and unfolding,
searching for something to wear for someone
who was no one, who had already gone.
I made notes of all the things I would say:
the kingfishers I'd seen on the Forest,
a mating pair, two more for your long list.
I went to parties, frittered time away.

Looking back, what hurts more than the knowing
is the not knowing. That this was the calm
before the gales and the wild, storm-blown rain –
the halcyon days that would now be mine
forever, would always carry my name.

New Meaning

after Thucydides

So then terms changed and words took new meaning:
frenzied recklessness we now called courage,
to think and wait, no more than sabotage,
seeing both sides we deemed doing nothing.
Friends who urged caution were the enemy.
Self-harm was our means of self-protection,
self-pity became self-preservation –
all that seemed certain was uncertainty.
Heart deposed head in coup and countercoup.
We stopped trusting, we used any weapon
to hand as the world split between those who
knew our pain and those who had it to come.
We felt raw, blooded, as this fixed turmoil
became our new state, seeped across our world.

Snow

after Homer

Out of nowhere, it flurries thick and fast,
early winter yet sharp as arrow shaft.
The wind calms. Grief is stilled. But it falls on
veiling the Forest hills, dark, distant Downs,
levelling fresh-ploughed farmland. By the church
it pales the priest's black coat as he clears paths
in vain, ghosts the bonnet of skidded hearse;
it dampens down crematorium furnace,
cuts off caterers, blocks would-be mourners.
Drifting further, across the south and west,
flakes catch on harbour walls like drying nets.
Now only the spray curved above Penzance
remains unblanched, grazed against those grey shores.
All else is wrapped in snow, stifled, silenced.

Glove

Among the scraps we find an outstanding
order, processed, which doesn't know to stop.
A week later, an oblong package drops
through the letterbox like some fresh offering
for the dead. Inside there's a pair of gloves,
black fleece, as if she had known we'd need them;
that this deep, early fall would be coming.
I scrunch my hand to find they fit, if snug,
and feel, once again, hers in mine, reaching
out to hold me safe, long past my childhood,
on main roads or slippery paths, guiding
me on as I laughed her off. Now I would
do anything to reach back, keep that hold
clasped round the unchanged centre of my world.

Frost

after Hesiod

A hard day, so raw it could flay an ox.
As our black procession finally tracked
north across the lanes, we breathed out frost
until the fields and Forest seemed to crack.
Now the leaves on oaks and pines were silvered
into good luck charms; below, hares shivered,
voles sighed in their sleep. Deer curled in coverts,
antlers quivering. I dreamed of hot baths,
of her sheepskin still on its cupboard hook.

But too soon we had pulled out of the woods.
Backs bent, twisted out like skidding wheel shafts,
the hunched pall bearers took their chilly hold.
Behind, my father inched on sticks, head bowed,
towards the chapel through the burning cold.

Ice

after Livy

All winter the earth tipped from under us;
we were balancing on sheer precipice,
with no way down or up. Beneath our feet
new snow had drifted on old, not too deep
yet soft, and the more we tried to progress,
the more it shrunk, the more it smoothed to slush
or compacted ice. Even if we crawled
on hands and knees, still we would falter, fall
without roots to cling on to, straws to hold,
each step an unyielding struggle. Below,
between the clouds, we saw our Forest streams,
the Downs lit by lowered sun; there, it seemed,
most lived their lives on solid, fertile ground.
For now we were trapped. Out of reach. Ice-bound.

Watch

Every day measures the same as the next...

A few months later my father spread out
some boxes on their bed – the jewellery
we'd helped him pick for anniversaries
and birthdays that we'd now no longer count.
I chose a pair of blue agate studs, sky
blanched, sea-washed, like her eyes. And her gold watch
so that I could still feel those same hours tick
on and on, the strict time that she'd lived by.
I wanted to think of her keeping score
of each lost second, holding that cold face
to the ear for one more, and then one more;
its hushed, imperceptible breath lasting
without end, nudging us back into place –
the soothing sound of her time still passing.

Turquoise

Another box opened like a triptych:
inside, looped like her smile, an amulet
of turquoise. I'd sent to Cornwall for it –
a thank you for that summer she'd reset
my own shattered heart; the stones that protect,
her new talisman, a charm to tempt fate
against some unknown harm or sudden death.
I remember how she'd leapt up, her face
caught in their sheen, still just semi-precious –
the wearing to come, the links to treasure.
I hang them round my neck, the searing touch
that had cured me once but could not guard her;
the shock of a Mount's Bay wave, its cold kiss
like flattened speech or thought suppressed: *What if...*

Thaw

after Livy

By now we were discouraged, exhausted.
We had set up camp on that same high ridge
yet were still on thin ice, with snow to dig
if we wanted to edge down, inch by inch.

And so we waited for the wind to change.
We stripped out dead undergrowth, gathered fuel,
used our bitterness to dissolve rock, flame
the glowing bracken and scorch a way through.

Turning back on ourselves, we eased the steep
gradients of the Forest, and then pushed
on round the valley slopes until we reached
the stream below in the shade of the woods.

Here we rested. At last this seemed somewhere
we could live. A softer landscape, gentler.

Spring

after Ibycus

Then it was Spring. In my parents' garden
the crab-apple tree foamed into blossom
like a river in full torrent. Across
the Weald new vines crept into bud, shaded
by tendril shoots; violets were weighted
down by dew in grass-tangled hedgerows, gorse
burned the heaths as if rekindled passion.

But our endless ache followed no season.
It had no respite or fresh beginnings;
a sudden April storm, stark sheet lightning
scorching the skies, or an abrupt north wind
stirring up withered leaves, so this longing
remained pitiless, bruising, black as blood,
crushing our hearts again from the ground up.

Street View

I click the cursor, pan in. By the kerb
a red Mini Cooper is parked, askew.
Even if plates are blurred, I know it's hers;
that May afternoon the cameras moved
through the verges of our shadowed landscape
as we gossip, walk the dog, hit the shops –
the humdrum, day on day chores we all take
for granted, can't believe will ever stop,
now virtually preserved. On the pavement
I shift down arrows, inch along the line,
as if I could track not just space but time;
could drag myself back to that lost moment
before she grabs her bag, locks the car door,
runs up the path to ring my bell once more.

Fairfield Church

Our last trip. We were laughing as she picked
her way across the causeway in high heels
and smart suit. *Well, we're going for a meal...*
Below, the marsh channels coiled like the Styx
by which even our gods swear faith; the rust
that can break glass or stone, that will corrode
not just hard iron or lead but pearl and bones.

This time all the birds of Kent and Sussex
have fallen silent as if Avernus,
the poisoned gate to Hell, lay beneath us.
Blocking the way a few miles up the road
we find them all: a vast murder of crows,
their black wings locking like a drawbridge grill
as they rise up, screeching, to let us through.

Breaking the Pact

after Virgil

Pass through its gates in darkness thick as fog
on a St Just morning. Here souls surge on;
starlings over the marsh at Marazion
rattled up by sharp winter squalls to blot
the parchment skies beyond. And still they come,
hemmed in by Styx's slime: slight youths, great men,
little girls – and mothers too, hearts broken.
But your songs can bring blood to ghosts, can numb
Furies, hush hounds of Hell, stem Ixion's wheel
and call her out, the soul you have to steal.
In this new madness of grief, don't look back,
don't follow in her steps. Don't break the pact
of the living and dead as time expires.
She will vanish like smoke from damped-down fire.

By-pass

after Plato

I knew the place already. Even if
for a second, I had been there myself
as my own heart was stopped and then started
again, healed. Perhaps that was why we failed,
could only grasp at the shadows of those
we had come to save, taking the coward's
quest – or the poet's – seeking out pathos,
regret's raw matter, not willing to die
in our turn: tricksters who'd somehow contrived
a way to quit the gates of Hell alive.

So the gods sent punishment we deserved;
this quagmire grief that serves as its own curse.
The pain you cannot write through or by-pass.
That feels like too little love. Or too much.

The Long Break

In Paris or Rome I would queue for hours,
in each PO until a booth was free,
my panic rising while its slot devoured
coin after sinking coin. Then, finally,
I'd hear her voice, faint as a far-struck stone
hitting water. And all my homesickness
would ripple out when she answered the phone
in her clipped voice like some resting actress.
I'd see her sitting on her pulled-out chair,
ankles crossed, legs twisted around – just where
she would have been on that last time we spoke;
the unfamiliar hiss then clack-clack-clack,
the soft drop of her *Hello?* echoed back
like a reclaimed sigh or a loss revoked.

Forfeit

after Hesiod

These are promises no one can foreswear.
Even the gods who break their faith will pay
full forfeit: one year of not drawing air
or taking breath, barely able to say
a word or speak a name. Of foregone feasts,
no pleasure in wine. Of dark months in bed,
hunched under the sheets as lethargy creeps
up and on, a hard ball of crushing lead.
But after long months of constant anguish
still to come is an even greater curse:
shunned company, poor counsel, lost friendships
until nine, maybe ten, whole years have passed...

And then slowly, slowly, the weight will lift.
Such is the oath all must make on the Styx.

Market Overton

Autumn. And death still catches up with us.
As notes recede from a just-stopped organ
we turn in sharp behind an emptied hearse.
Under watched clock, we find the stretched warden:
after today there are just thirty plots
left but, if you don't mind, I must close up...
Shadows scar the tower. Snarling gargoyles
are mottled by horse chestnut, rashed with yew.
Beyond the trampled grass, a slant-faced stile
leans back into the light, pulling us through;
a few more stone-smoothed steps from field to grave,
each mourned as we now mourn – those *ifs* and *shoulds*
winding back to heap of earth, flash of spade.
The soft, relentless hiss of soil on wood.

The Other Path

In my dream you were still here, up ahead
in your best hat and coat. *It's Jo* I said
as you turned round, perplexed, testing the word
on your tongue as if one you'd never heard
but knew you should remember. *Jo? Ah. Yes.*
Pale as a splintered moon scudding through clouds
we catch – or think we catch – at falling dusk,
you were frowning, flinty, a stranger cast
in Penwith granite. I woke drenched in sweat,
back from the Underworld like Aeneas
stepping out of the sedge and dank morass.
Now I saw that here was the other path
you might have taken the night you left us.
The one that would have splintered all our hearts.

Roman Road

Camp Hill. Clouds taut as guy-ropes tether land
to sky, steadying the heart. *The way up,*
as Heraclitus taught, *is the way down...*
Horses gallop past, churning up the scrub
on the road to Rome. *The dead are our friends,*
our colleagues, our fellow conspirators.
They, too, shape our waking world... Loss and gain.
Conquest and defeat. The spurred messengers
bringing word from each broken side. The same
time yet in a different time. Here it seems
those endless lines might cross and cross again.

A crow startles. Sheep rest on the heaped edge
as if warmed by hidden bones. *Still we dream*
our own locked dreams, the living and the dead.

Friends

Now the moon is its own half-skeleton
half-etched above the clump, Downs a far blur.
By the path there are wilted carnations
and a soaked card from another daughter
who cannot bear to walk these lanes alone –
the muddy debris of unwound despair,
folded in with birdsong like a struck stone.
When time is torn how can it be repaired?
If we held out our hands could we still touch?
A different time but at the same time. Past
and present. *The way down is the way up.*
A grazing deer takes measure. Could we pass
and know? Could we pass unknown? *Existence
keeps its secrets.* Who we are. Where we went.

The Way Down

These walks are where I find you. Observance.
Now grief is absence where there was presence,
chill where there was warmth. Every morning,
each day, the waking and remembering,
the remembering on waking. The sigh
of knowing and of not knowing. *We die*
in each other's life, live each other's death...

Among the ghost-trees of this once-Forest
I know that you are still at my shoulder,
walking by my side but on a different
day in a different time. Here if not here.
Time will move on, flow in its own current.
What the dead leave for the living, their gift:
the pleasure in the moment. A life lived.

Cleft

By a cliff top path where the grass is pressed
like the imprint of lovers' morning hair
or faded graveyard cross, there is a cleft –
Mary's word – that in Virgil or Homer
would lead to the Underworld, Erebus:
grief, disease, the horrors of its darkness,
but here is stopped by a sprig of late thrift,
a faded kiss to keep us from the brink.

At Botallack the mist slides out from field
and sea, infinity slowly revealed,
our own world returned, piece by fragile piece –
a place to stop the hurt, to lease back speech;
this necromancer's task of easing breath
into moss-flecked lungs of our long, long dead.

The Road To St Just

There were clouds like fallen angels, wings shed
and heads bowed, over the brow of Carn Brea.
Or a watchful mother by child's sick bed
softly keeping vigil, barring the way:
I believe we all have a guardian
to stand by us you'd said. At Marazion
the Mount turned blood-red for Remembrance Day,
an upturned chalice on brimmed, star-stepped bay.

Trailed by the moon on the road to St Just,
my shuddering car became alchemist
transforming mud to quick-silver, fool's gold;
if I'd driven on to Land's End, from east
to west and back, I'd have forged a halo
to ring us around, kept you safe myself.

Seat

Even from the bench, the bay is undimmed;
beyond hazy blackthorn the Mount quivers
as its pine trees tilt, reeled back by the wind –
the marker that tells us we're really here
at the far point, lying low, facing west.
Below, rocks snag across a land on loan
from the turning tide, shrunk into darkness.
Nothing soothes the soul like the sight of home:
this one rears daughters fierce as fighting men.
Here's where you rested with your own mother
watching swifts dip, dissect the setting sun,
by paths picked out in selfheal and clover.
Blood and bone pack the sacred ground beneath:
your place. My longed-for Ithaca. Our seat.

Let Go

after Virgil

Those nights I called her name in vain again
and again, filled ruined cities with tears.
I dreamt I reached familiar streets, my fear
fixing tongue to roof of mouth, hair on end;
again she came to me through parted crowds,
smarter than ever in weathershield mac,
blood red lipstick and jaunty, matching hat
like a warrior plume. 'I can't stay long now,'
she said, 'yet am always here. Remember
to hold your hopes close, guard your ambition.
Love. Travel. Most of all, let go anger
or this exile of grief will be too long.'
I tried and tried and tried to embrace her
but, like a thought on waking, she was gone.

Star

So we come full circle to falling dusk.
Above Priest's Cove, the sky is darkening
through Brisons rocks, evening hesitating
between clouds and sea, cautious, on the cusp.
A shard of moon slips through, blurred with regret,
fresh votive to this place, our penitence
for the lost: parents, old friends and the house
we mourned as if a lover rashly left.

But the day has gone, its turning point passed.
Now the most beautiful of all the stars –
the evening star, shepherd star, Hesperus –
gathers all that light-tinged dawn has scattered;
it guides the fishing boats, herds in sailors,
sends daughters running home to their mothers.

.

Gemini

Every year, on the day, she'd recall the scent
of mown grass, her gas and air; white sheets
pegged across the line like a field-hospital tent.
How she called to neighbours over gull shrieks
and how, on a June lawn, a month too soon,

I was exiled, pushed from the womb
by my own, unexpected mirror image,
sending me first, gifting me life instead.
After, my father took the other out for burial,
wrapped in brown paper like an unsent parcel.

This year, there will be no retold story –
nothing but a leaf frail, the trace of her
flesh in ours; a scar of earth another family
will long ago have turned over, disturbed
to plant peonies or roses, pale as new-born skin,

petal linked to petal, each fresh symmetry
unfolding in the sun like a new-born twin.

Sources and notes:

p.11. Things We Leave Behind:
after *The Afternoon Sun* by C.P. Cavafy.

p.13. Lost:
after Virgil, Aeneid, 2.735-57.
(As Troy falls to the Greeks, the fleeing Trojan prince Aeneas realises that his wife, Creusa, is missing.)

p.14. Suppliants:
lines 4-14 trace Aeschylus, *Suppliant Women,*180-202.
(In Aeschylus's Greek tragedy, the 50 daughters of Danaus, known as the Danaides, flee forced marriages in Egypt to seek sanctuary in the Greek city of Argos; on landing, Danaus sees a welcoming party advancing towards them, unsure if it is hostile or friendly.)

p.17 Halcyon:
after Ovid, *Metamorphoses,*11. 573-82.
(Halcyone – or Alcyone – was unaware that her husband, Ceyx, had been drowned at sea until his ghost appeared to her in a dream. On finding his body washed up on the shore, she threw herself in the waves and was turned into a kingfisher, named halcyone after her, as were the 'halcyon days' of the calm, mid-winter seas when the birds are said to lay their nests.)

p.18. New Meaning:
after Thucydides, *The Peloponnesian War,* 3. 82-4.
(In 427 BCE, during the long war between Athens and Sparta, the Athenians' ally Corcyra suffers constant political revolutions and internal strife leading to stasis as various factions in the state jostle for power.)

p.19. Snow:
after Homer, *Iliad,*12.278-86.
(Homer's epic simile compares the missiles of the Greeks raining down on a besieged Troy to snow falling across the land.)

p.21. Frost:
after Hesiod, *Works And Days,* 504-535.
(Hesiod's ancient farmers' almanac, written around 700 BCE, here describes wintry weather.)

p.22. Ice:
after Livy, *History of Rome,* 21.36-7
(During Hannibal's march on Rome in 218 BCE, the Carthaginian troops become trapped on an impassable precipice in the snowbound Alps.)

p.23. Watch:
title quote from Heraclitus fragment 106.

p.25. Thaw:
after Livy, *History of Rome,* 21, 37.
(Hannibal's troops at last find a way down from the Alps by clearing paths in the snow and melting rockfalls with brushwood fires, adding vinegar from their rations to degrade the stones before hacking a way through to lower ground.)

p.26. Spring:
after Ibycus PMG 286.
(For the sixth century BCE poet, the new beginnings of spring bring only fresh pain.)

p.28. Fairfield Church:
lines 5-7 after Pausanias, *Description of Greece,* 8.18.5.
Lake Avernus in southern Italy, whose name means 'birdless', is said to be the entrance to the Underworld.
Fairfield Church is an isolated chapel on Romney Marsh, near Rye, East Sussex.

p.29. Breaking the Pact:
after Virgil, *Georgics,* 4.467-500.
(The poet Orpheus travels down to the Underworld to retrieve his dead wife, Eurydice; the beauty of his songs sways Hades, king of the dead, to allow her to return on the condition that Orpheus does not look back at her as they walk towards the living world. But he cannot resist and glances round to see her vanishing again into the realms of the dead.)

p.30. By-pass:
after Plato, *Symposium,* 179d.
(Plato accuses Orpheus of cowardice since, rather than dying in his wife's place, he attempted to return alive from the Underworld with Eurydice.)

p.32. Forfeit:
after Hesiod, *Theogony,* 793-804.
(Hesiod describes how the gods swear their binding oaths on the Styx, the river of the Underworld.)

p.33 Market Overton:
A village in Rutland.

p.34. The Other Path:
lines 6-11 after Virgil *Aeneid,* 6. 452-4 & 469-71.
(As Aeneas descends to the Underworld to find the ghost of his dead father Anchises, he meets the ghost of his lover, Dido, queen of Carthage, who committed suicide after he abandoned her to sail on towards Italy and Rome.)

p.35. Roman Road:
embedded quotes from Heraclitus fragments 60, 75 & 89.
A part of the London-Lewes Roman road is visible near Camp Hill clump on the
Ashdown Forest, East Sussex.

p.36. Friends:
embedded quotes from Heraclitus fragments 60 &123.
Friends is a clump of trees on the Ashdown Forest.

p.37. The Way Down:
embedded quote from Heraclitus fragment 62.

p.38. Cleft:
inspired by a photograph by Alistair Common.
Botallack is a coastal mining village in west Cornwall.

p.39. The Road to St Just:
Chapel Carn Brea (pronounced 'Bray') is a granite outcrop between St Just-in-
Penwith and Land's End in west Cornwall.
St Michael's Mount, a tiny island off Marazion in Mount's Bay, is often abbreviated
locally to 'the Mount'.

p.40. Seat:
lines 1-8 are after Homer, *Odyssey*, 9.21-8.
(At the court of the Phaeacian king, Alcinous, Odysseus speaks of his longing for
his homeland Ithaca.)
The seat is on the costal footpath between Marazion and Perranuthnoe.

p.41. Let Go:
after Virgil, *Aeneid*, 2.768-94.
(As Aeneas desperately searches Troy for his missing wife, Creusa's ghost appears
to him, telling him to move on to Rome without her.)

p.42. Star:
lines 10-14 from Sappho fragments 104b & 104a
(based on my translations in *Sappho: Poems & Fragments* p.82.)
Priest's Cove is below Cape Cornwall near St Just-in-Penwith in west Cornwall.

p.45. Gemini:
This poem was written for the *Agenda* special edition in honour of John Burnside
(*Dwelling Places: An Appreciation of John Burnside,* 45.4/46.1, Spring 2011).